MARINADES
&
RUBS

LOVE FOOD

Love Food™ is an imprint of Parragon Books Ltd

Parragon
Queen Street House
4 Queen Street
Bath BA1 1HE, UK

Text by Carol Wilson
Designed by Terry Jeavons & Company
Photographer: Mike Cooper
Home economist: Lincoln Jefferson.

ISBN 978-1-4054-8773-3

Printed in China

This book uses imperial, metric, and US cup measurements. Follow the same units of measurement
throughout; do not mix imperial and metric. All spoon measurements are level, unless otherwise stated:
teaspoons are assumed to be 5ml, and tablespoons are assumed to be 15ml. Unless otherwise stated,
milk is assumed to be whole, eggs and individual fruits such as bananas are medium, and pepper is
freshly ground black pepper.

Recipes using raw or very lightly cooked eggs should be avoided by infants, the elderly, pregnant
women, convalescents, and anyone suffering from an illness. Pregnant and breast-feeding women are
advised to avoid eating peanuts and peanut products.

Contents

Introduction

Marinades and rubs are a great way of adding flavor to all types of food, and are speedy and simple to prepare, they need only to be left for a while to work their magic in advance of cooking.

Mouthwatering Marinades

A marinade is a liquid or paste used to soak foods before cooking. It helps to tenderize meat, game, poultry, and fish and seafood, thus reducing the cooking time, and adds moisture, ensuring that the food remains succulent.

Rubs are the dry equivalent of marinades and form a coating on the outside of food to add extra flavor without extra moisture, and without overpowering the natural taste of the food.

The best marinades have a subtle balance of acid (citrus juices or vinegar), oil, and flavorings, such as spices, herbs, and citrus rind—acid tenderizes food, while the oil lubricates it. Many marinades contain sweet ingredients, such as sugar, honey, or fruit juice. The sugars on the surface of the food caramelize when exposed to heat, resulting in an attractive brown color and deep flavor. Some marinades contain yogurt, which is mildly acidic and therefore ideal for tenderizing tough cuts of meat. Asian recipes often use yogurt marinades for lamb and goat.

Always choose the best-quality ingredients for marinades. Fine oils and vinegars will give much better results than cheap, inferior varieties. Experiment with different oils, such as sesame, walnut, hazelnut (make sure that no one has a nut allergy before using), and different olive oils; French, Greek, Spanish, and Italian olive oils each have different characteristics and flavors. Likewise, a traditionally made and aged balsamic vinegar, for instance, with its complex qualities, will make all the difference to the flavor of a dish. Other vinegars to try are rice, red or white wine, sherry, and apple cider. There are also interesting fruit vinegars available, such as raspberry and fig, or herb-infused vinegars.

Food should be submerged in the marinade and turned from time to time to ensure that the flavors are absorbed evenly. Don't be tempted to marinate food for longer than stated in a recipe—some marinades, particularly those containing plain yogurt or lemon juice, soften meat and fish, which, if marinated for too long, will become mushy. As a general rule, fish needs 2–3 hours marinating, while meat can be marinated for up to 24 hours, depending on the actual marinade. When the flavors are allowed to stand and mingle, cold marinated dishes taste even better the next day. If you are marinating food for longer than a couple of hours, avoid adding too much salt, citrus juice, or vinegar, as these have the effect of "cooking" the food being marinated.

Remarkable Rubs

A rub consists of a mixture of dry herbs and/or spices, salt and/or sugar, and is rubbed into raw food just before, if short of time, or for a few hours before cooking and up to 24 hours ahead for a more intense flavor. As the food cooks and releases its juices, the flavor is absorbed into the food, leaving a coating on the outside. Work rubs into food thoroughly and, if using poultry, under the skin, too. The longer the coated food stands, the better in order to allow the flavors to mingle and be absorbed.

Rubs made up of dry ingredients keep extremely well, so you can make up a batch and store it in a clean, dry container with a tight-fitting lid. However, avoid storing rub mixtures for more than three months, as the spices will begin to lose flavor. Whether you are a kitchen novice or an experienced cook, you will be fascinated to discover how much you can vary the flavor of all sorts of foods by using different complementary marinades and rubs, so enjoy using these easy recipes to pep up your cooking.

Mouthwatering Marinades

Experience a whole range of flavor sensations in this comprehensive collection of marinades, from the smoky, fiery punch of Chipotle Marinade to the citrusy tang of Key Lime Marinade. Along with the classic Sticky Barbecue Marinade there are some more surprising ideas, including the sweet yet piquant Coca-Cola Marinade and the Spanish-Style Marinade made with Seville bitter orange marmalade and juice. Alcohol not only flavors but tenderizes—tequila, teamed with lime and chile, provides a distinctive Mexican quality, and dark rum, combined with warm spices and brown sugar, gives a taste of the Caribbean. Also featured are the characteristic flavors of other favorite cuisines, such as Thai, Indian, Japanese, and Chinese.

Always marinate food in a nonmetallic dish or in a plastic food bag, and don't use foil. Resist the temptation to marinate for longer than stated, as the food will become too soft. Marinated food may be broiled, cooked in a grill pan, pan-fried, barbecued, roasted, or oven-baked for the usual length of cooking time.

Sticky Barbecue Marinade

¼ cup light or dark brown sugar

5 tbsp plum preserve

2 tbsp tomato paste

2 tbsp white wine vinegar

1 tbsp wholegrain mustard

Makes enough for about
1 lb 2 oz/500 g meat, poultry,
or fish and seafood

1 Heat all the ingredients in a pan over low heat, stirring until smooth. Remove from the heat and let cool.

2 Meanwhile, score the meat, poultry, or fish portions deeply with a sharp knife. Put the prepared meat, poultry, or fish in a shallow nonmetallic dish or plastic food bag.

3 Pour the marinade over the prepared meat, poultry, or fish, and turn to coat.

4 Cover tightly or seal and let marinate in the refrigerator, turning occasionally, for at least an hour or preferably, for meat only, overnight before cooking.

TASTY TIP
Especially good with pork spareribs, sausages, or chicken, this tasty marinade cooks to a gloriously sticky, flavorsome coating. Try using other types of preserves, such as apricot preserve or red currant preserve, or marmalade for an orangey flavor.

Tex-Mex Marinade

³/₄ cup tomato ketchup

1 tbsp freshly squeezed lemon or lime juice

1 tsp Tabasco sauce

1 tsp ground cumin

1 tsp salt

¹/₂ tsp pepper

Makes enough for about
1 lb 2 oz/500 g meat, poultry,
or fish and seafood

1 Score the meat, poultry, or fish portions deeply with a sharp knife. Put the prepared meat, poultry, fish, or seafood, in a shallow nonmetallic dish or plastic food bag.

2 Mix all the ingredients together in a pitcher or small bowl until thoroughly combined. Pour the marinade over the prepared meat, poultry, fish, or seafood, and turn to coat.

3 Cover tightly or seal and let marinate in the refrigerator, turning occasionally, for up to 2 hours for fish and seafood or up to 24 hours for meat and poultry before cooking.

TASTY TIP
This delicious and lively marinade is guaranteed to bring a touch of Mexican magic to any of your favorite foods—and it is especially recommended for use with meat dishes such as barbecued or broiled chicken, sausages, and pork spareribs.

Chipotle Marinade

6 canned chipotle chiles, drained and 2 tsp juices or sauce from the can, reserved

3 ripe plum tomatoes

1/2 cup freshly squeezed lime juice

1/2 cup freshly squeezed orange juice

2 tbsp white wine vinegar

2 garlic cloves

1 tsp dried oregano

1 tsp salt

1 tsp pepper

Makes enough for about 1 lb 8 oz/675 g meat, poultry, or fish and seafood

1 Score the meat, poultry, or fish portions deeply with a sharp knife. Put the prepared meat, poultry, fish, or seafood in a shallow nonmetallic dish or plastic food bag.

2 Put all the ingredients in a food processor or blender and process until smooth and combined.

3 Pour the marinade over the prepared meat, poultry, fish, or seafood and turn to coat.

4 Cover tightly or seal and let marinate in the refrigerator, turning occasionally, for up to 2 hours for fish and seafood, 6 hours for poultry, and 12 hours for meat before cooking.

TASTY TIP
The chipotle chiles lend a rich, smoky heat to this powerful marinade, which can be used for meat dishes such as beef steaks, chicken, pork, or fish and seafood. Chipotle chiles are jalapeño chiles that have been smoke-dried and they pack a fiery punch!

Red Chile and Herb Marinade

2 fresh red chiles, seeded and chopped

1 garlic clove, crushed

2–3 tbsp chopped fresh herbs of your choice

4 tbsp white wine vinegar

2 tbsp sunflower oil

1 tbsp superfine sugar

1 tsp pepper

1/2 tsp salt

Makes enough for about 1 lb 2 oz/500 g meat, poultry, or fish and seafood

1 Score the meat, poultry, or fish portions deeply with a sharp knife. Put the prepared meat, poultry, fish, or seafood in a shallow nonmetallic dish or plastic food bag.

2 Mix all the ingredients together in a pitcher or small bowl until thoroughly combined. Pour the marinade over the prepared meat, poultry, fish, or seafood and turn to coat.

3 Cover tightly or seal and let marinate in the refrigerator, turning occasionally, for up to 2 hours before cooking.

TASTY TIP
A hot, but not fiery, marinade that goes well with most meats, poultry, fish and seafood, as well as vegetables, such as squash wedges or new potatoes, which can then be roasted. You can use any herbs you like—a single herb, such as rosemary, or a mixture of herbs—to vary the flavor.

Mexican Tequila Marinade

1/2 cup freshly squeezed lime juice

4 tbsp tequila

2 tbsp vegetable oil

2 tsp finely grated lime rind

1 tsp dried oregano

1 tsp salt

1/2–1 tsp chili powder

Makes enough for about 1 lb 8 oz/675 g meat, poultry, or fish and seafood

1 Mix all the ingredients together in a nonmetallic pitcher or small bowl until thoroughly combined. Cover and let stand at room temperature for about 20 minutes.

2 Meanwhile, score the meat, poultry, or fish portions deeply with a sharp knife. Put the prepared meat, poultry, fish, or seafood in a shallow nonmetallic dish or plastic food bag.

3 Pour the marinade over the prepared meat, poultry, fish, or seafood and turn to coat.

4 Cover tightly or seal and let marinate in the refrigerator, turning occasionally, for 1–3 hours for meat and poultry or 30 minutes for fish and seafood. Drain, reserving the marinade, but don't pat dry before cooking.

5 Bring the reserved marinade to a boil in a small pan and boil rapidly for 5 minutes. Drizzle over the cooked meat, poultry, or fish and seafood just before serving.

TASTY TIP
The flavor of the oregano moderates the powerful taste of the tequila in this recipe. This recipe is particularly recommended for marinating any poultry or fish and seafood dish, such as monkfish, shrimp, or salmon and tomato kabobs.

Mojito Marinade

4 garlic cloves

1 fresh serrano chile or large fresh red chile, seeded or not to taste

2 tbsp finely chopped onion

4 tbsp freshly squeezed orange juice

2 tbsp freshly squeezed lime juice

finely grated rind of 1 lime

4 tbsp olive oil

2 tbsp white rum

2 tbsp light brown sugar

1 tsp ground cumin

1 tsp pepper

¹/₂ tsp salt

1 tsp chopped fresh oregano

1 tbsp chopped fresh cilantro

1 tbsp chopped fresh mint

Makes enough for about 2 lb/900 g meat, poultry, or fish and seafood

1 Score the meat, poultry, or fish portions deeply with a sharp knife. Put the prepared meat, poultry, fish, or seafood in a shallow nonmetallic dish or plastic food bag.

2 Put all the ingredients in a food processor or blender and process until smooth and combined.

3 Pour the marinade over the prepared meat, poultry, fish, or seafood and turn to coat.

4 Cover tightly or seal and let marinate in the refrigerator, turning occasionally, for up to 2 hours before cooking.

TASTY TIP
This marinade recipe is based on the popular Cuban cocktail and will keep for up to two weeks in the refrigerator. It is the perfect accompaniment to pork, chicken, or vegetables, but is especially good when used with baked salmon, garnished with lime and mint.

Bourbon and Herb Marinade

1/2 cup olive oil

4 tbsp bourbon

3 tbsp white wine vinegar

3 garlic cloves

1 small onion, sliced

1 tbsp Dijon mustard

1 tsp fresh oregano leaves

1 tsp fresh sage leaves

1 tsp fresh rosemary leaves

1 tsp fresh thyme leaves

Makes enough for about
1 lb 2 oz/500 g meat, poultry,
or fish and seafood

1 Score the meat, poultry, or fish portions deeply with a sharp knife. Put the prepared meat, poultry, fish, or seafood in a shallow nonmetallic dish or plastic food bag.

2 Put all the ingredients in a food processor or blender and process until smooth and combined.

3 Pour the marinade over the prepared meat, poultry, fish, or seafood and turn to coat.

4 Cover tightly or seal and let marinate in the refrigerator, turning occasionally, for up to 2 hours before cooking.

TASTY TIP
Add a zing to meat, poultry, fish, seafood, and vegetables, such as chunks of corncob, bell peppers, or zucchini, with this mild marinade. Use any type of whiskey you may have in place of the bourbon. Prepared English mustard or wholegrain mustard can be substituted for the Dijon mustard.

Spicy Beer Marinade

1¹/₂ cups beer

generous ¹/₃ cup soy sauce

1 tbsp Worcestershire sauce

1 tsp Tabasco sauce

1 garlic clove, finely chopped

1 tbsp wholegrain mustard

2 tsp paprika

1 tsp salt

1 tsp pepper

Makes enough for about 1 lb 2 oz/500 g meat or game

1 Score the meat or game portions deeply with a sharp knife. Put the prepared meat or game in a shallow nonmetallic dish or plastic food bag.

2 Whisk all the ingredients together in a pitcher or small bowl until thoroughly combined.

3 Pour the marinade over the prepared meat or game and turn to coat.

4 Cover tightly or seal and let marinate in the refrigerator, turning occasionally, for up to 6 hours before cooking.

TASTY TIP
This gutsy marinade goes particularly well with beef, venison, and wild boar, the beer making it wonderfully tender as well as flavorsome. You can use any beer for this appetizing marinade. A dark beer will give a more powerful flavor, while a lager will produce milder results.

Coca-Cola Marinade

1¹/₂ cups Coca-Cola or
Cherry Coke, not Diet Coke

2 tbsp vegetable oil

2 tbsp Worcestershire sauce

2 tbsp tomato ketchup

1 tbsp prepared mild mustard

1 garlic clove, crushed

salt and pepper

Makes enough for about
1 lb 8 oz/675 g meat or poultry

1 Score the meat or poultry portions deeply with a sharp knife. Put the prepared meat or poultry in a shallow nonmetallic dish or plastic food bag.

2 Whisk all the ingredients together in a pitcher or small bowl until thoroughly combined.

3 Pour the marinade over the prepared meat or poultry, and turn to coat.

4 Cover tightly or seal and let marinate in the refrigerator, turning occasionally, for up to 6 hours before cooking.

TASTY TIP
Coca-Cola or Cherry Coke makes a surprising and fabulous sweet marinade for all manner of meat, including pork spareribs, and poultry, such as grilled chicken wings. Don't be tempted to use Diet Coke—the sugar in Coca-Cola is necessary to caramelize the food.

Key Lime Marinade

**finely grated rind and juice of
2 Key limes**

**finely grated rind and juice of
1 lemon**

1 tbsp chopped fresh mint

1 tbsp honey

1 tbsp olive oil

1 tsp ground coriander

1 tsp paprika

1 tsp ground cumin

**Makes enough for about
1 lb 2 oz/500 g meat, poultry,
or fish and seafood**

1 Score the meat, poultry, or fish portions deeply with a sharp knife. Put the prepared meat, poultry, fish, or seafood in a shallow nonmetallic dish or plastic food bag.

2 Mix all the ingredients together in a pitcher or small bowl until thoroughly combined.

3 Pour the marinade over the prepared meat, poultry, fish, or seafood and turn to coat.

4 Cover tightly or seal and let marinate in the refrigerator, turning occasionally, for up to 2 hours before cooking.

TASTY TIP
This ultra-citrusy marinade is perfect for chicken, fish, and seafood. The Key lime, from Florida, is also known as the Mexican lime or West Indian lime and is more acidic and tart than the more common Persian lime. You can also use Persian limes in this recipe, but you will only need the rind and juice from one fruit instead of two.

Thai-Style Marinade

finely grated rind and
juice of 2 limes

1-inch/2.5-cm piece fresh
ginger root, peeled and grated

2 garlic cloves, crushed

1 bunch of fresh cilantro, leaves
and stems, finely chopped

3 tbsp olive oil

2 tsp salt

1 tsp pepper

$\frac{1}{2}$ tsp ground cumin

Makes enough for about
1 lb 8 oz/675 g meat, poultry,
or fish and seafood

1 Score the meat, poultry, or fish portions deeply with a sharp knife. Put the prepared meat, poultry, fish, or seafood in a shallow nonmetallic dish or plastic food bag.

2 Mix all the ingredients together in a pitcher or small bowl until thoroughly combined.

3 Pour the marinade over the prepared meat, poultry, fish, or seafood and turn to coat.

4 Cover tightly or seal and let marinate in the refrigerator, turning occasionally, for up to 2 hours before cooking.

TASTY TIP
The enticing flavors of this marinade are typically Thai. The fragrant cilantro, lime, and ginger combine with spicy cumin, making it an ideal marinade to accompany any fish and seafood dishes, such as shrimp served on skewers, as well as chicken and pork.

Tandoori Yogurt Marinade

1 tsp chili powder

1 tsp ground turmeric

1 tsp ground cumin

1 tsp garam masala

1 tsp ground cinnamon

4 onions, finely chopped

2 garlic cloves, crushed

1¼ cups plain yogurt

juice of 2 lemons

5 tbsp sunflower or peanut oil

5 tbsp tomato paste

2 tbsp white or red wine vinegar

2 tbsp dark brown sugar

2 tsp grated fresh ginger root

salt and pepper

Makes enough for about
1 lb 2 oz/500 g meat, poultry,
or fish and seafood

1 Score the meat, poultry, or fish portions deeply with a sharp knife. Put the prepared meat, poultry, fish, or seafood in a shallow nonmetallic dish or plastic food bag.

2 Mix all the dry spices together in a pitcher or small bowl, then add all the remaining ingredients and stir until thoroughly combined.

3 Pour the marinade over the prepared meat, poultry, fish, or seafood and turn to coat.

4 Cover tightly or seal and let marinate in the refrigerator, turning occasionally, for up to 2 hours for fish and seafood or 4–6 hours, or overnight for meat and poultry before cooking.

TASTY TIP
This is a classic creamy Indian marinade, and provides just a hint of heat from the spices. It is an excellent marinade to enhance the flavors of broiled rack of lamb or a chicken dish. The name tandoori comes from the large Indian clay oven called a tandoor, where the marinated meat is cooked.

Asian Marinade

6 tbsp peanut oil

4 tbsp black bean sauce

4 tbsp rice wine

2 tbsp light soy sauce

2 garlic cloves, crushed

**1-inch/2.5-cm piece fresh
ginger root, peeled and
finely grated pepper**

**Makes enough for about
1 lb 2 oz/500 g meat, poultry,
or fish and seafood**

1 Score the meat, poultry, or fish portions deeply with a sharp knife. Put the prepared meat, poultry, fish, or seafood, in a shallow nonmetallic dish or plastic food bag.

2 Mix all the ingredients together in a pitcher or small bowl until thoroughly combined.

3 Pour the marinade over the prepared meat, poultry, fish, or seafood, and turn to coat.

4 Cover tightly or seal and let marinate in the refrigerator, turning occasionally, for 2–3 hours before cooking.

TASTY TIP
This exotically flavored marinade is excellent with pork, including spareribs, chicken, and roast duck breasts. The salty, spicy black bean sauce imparts a unique flavor. You can find jars of black bean sauce in Asian food stores or in larger grocery stores.

Teriyaki Marinade

¹/₂ cup dark soy sauce

scant 1 cup mirin (Japanese
sweet rice wine)

1 tbsp light brown sugar

Makes enough for about
1 lb 2 oz/500 g meat, poultry,
or fish and seafood

1 Score the meat, poultry, or fish portions deeply with a sharp knife. Put the prepared meat, poultry, fish, or seafood in a shallow nonmetallic dish or plastic food bag.

2 Heat all the ingredients in a large skillet over medium heat, stirring until the sugar has dissolved. Remove from the heat and let cool.

3 Pour the marinade over the prepared meat, poultry, fish, or seafood and turn to coat.

4 Cover tightly or seal and let marinate in the refrigerator, turning occasionally, for up to 24 hours before cooking.

TASTY TIP
This Japanese-style marinade is perfect for use with salmon and trout fillets, chicken, duck, and beef steaks. Mirin is a type of sweetened rice wine or sake, designed for use in cooking with a reduced alcohol content, but you can substitute a pale dry sherry if you cannot find it.

Chinese Five-Spice and Sherry Vinegar Marinade

5 tbsp soy sauce

4 tbsp medium sherry

3 tbsp sherry vinegar

3 tbsp sunflower oil

1 tbsp Chinese five-spice powder

1 tsp dark brown sugar

1 tsp ground ginger

1 garlic clove, crushed

Makes enough for about 1 lb 2 oz/500 g meat, poultry, or fish and seafood

1 Score the meat, poultry, or fish portions deeply with a sharp knife. Put the prepared poultry, meat, fish, or seafood, in a shallow nonmetallic dish or plastic food bag.

2 Mix all the ingredients together in a pitcher or small bowl until thoroughly combined.

3 Pour the marinade over the prepared poultry, meat, fish, or seafood, and turn to coat.

4 Cover tightly or seal and let marinate in the refrigerator, turning occasionally, for at least 3 hours, or preferably overnight before cooking.

TASTY TIP
A Chinese-style marinade that is great with chicken or duck portions, pork spareribs, or pork steaks. If you can find it, use Chinese rice wine in place of the sherry. You can also use sesame oil instead of sunflower oil for additional flavor.

Satay Marinade

¹/₂-inch/1-cm piece fresh ginger
root, peeled and grated

2 garlic cloves, crushed

1 cup coconut cream

4 tbsp roasted peanuts, finely
crushed

2 tbsp light soy sauce

1 tbsp honey

1 tbsp ground coriander

1 tsp ground cumin

1 tsp ground turmeric

Makes enough for about
1 lb 8 oz/675 g meat, poultry,
or fish and seafood

1 Score the meat, poultry, or fish portions deeply with a sharp knife. Put the prepared meat, poultry, fish, or seafood in a shallow nonmetallic dish or plastic food bag.

2 Mix all the ingredients together in a pitcher or small bowl until thoroughly combined.

3 Pour the marinade over the prepared meat, poultry, fish, or seafood and turn to coat.

4 Cover tightly or seal and let marinate in the refrigerator, turning occasionally, for at least 2 hours, or preferably overnight before cooking.

TASTY TIP
A creamy, spicy marinade that is ideal for vegetable or tofu skewers, or for chicken, beef, pork, or large shrimp. Coconut cream is available from Asian stores and large grocery stores. If you can't find it, pour off the thin liquid from an unshaken can of coconut milk and use the remaining thicker liquid.

Piri Piri Marinade

6 fresh red chiles

3 garlic cloves

generous 1/3 cup olive oil

4 tbsp freshly squeezed lemon juice

1/2 tsp dried oregano

1/2 tbsp paprika

1/2 tsp salt

Makes enough for about 1 lb 2 oz/500 g meat, poultry, or fish and seafood

1 Preheat the oven to 350°F/180°C.

2 Spread the chiles out on a cookie sheet and roast in the preheated oven for 10 minutes.

3 Let cool, cut off the stems, then transfer to a food processor or blender. Add all the remaining ingredients and process until smooth and combined.

4 Score the meat, poultry, or fish portions deeply with a sharp knife. Put the prepared meat, poultry, fish, or seafood in a shallow nonmetallic dish or plastic food bag.

5 Pour the marinade over the prepared meat, poultry, fish, or seafood and turn to coat.

6 Cover tightly or seal and let marinate in the refrigerator, turning occasionally, for at least 1 hour or up to 6 hours before cooking.

TASTY TIP
A fiery chile and garlic marinade that goes well with chicken, duck, pork, and shrimp. To moderate the heat, cut the roasted chiles in half and scrape out the seeds and membranes. Be careful, as the seeds and membranes can cause painful burning of the skin and eyes. It is advisable to wear gloves when handling.

Spanish-Style Marinade

¼ cup light brown sugar

5 tbsp Seville bitter orange marmalade

2 tbsp freshly squeezed Seville orange juice

2 tbsp tomato paste

1 tbsp wholegrain mustard

Makes enough for about 1 lb 2 oz/500 g meat, poultry, or fish and seafood

1 Score the meat, poultry, or fish portions deeply with a sharp knife. Put the prepared meat, poultry, fish, or seafood, in a shallow nonmetallic dish or plastic food bag.

2 Heat all the ingredients in a pan over low heat, stirring until smooth. Remove from the heat and let cool.

3 Pour the marinade over the prepared meat, poultry, fish, or seafood, and turn to coat.

4 Cover tightly or seal and let marinate in the refrigerator, turning occasionally, for up to 12 hours before cooking.

TASTY TIP
Highly scented bitter Seville oranges with their fragrant peel and sharp juice are the perfect complements for duck, chicken, pork spareribs, lamb, and fish steaks, such as tuna. Don't use sweet oranges. If you can't find Seville oranges, use 1 tablespoon sweet orange juice with 1 tablespoon lemon juice.

Argentinian Chimichurri Marinade

1/2 cup white wine vinegar

3 tbsp olive oil

2 fresh jalapeño chiles, seeded or not to taste

2 garlic cloves

1 tsp paprika

1 tsp salt

1/2 tsp ground bay leaves

1 tbsp chopped fresh cilantro

1 tbsp chopped fresh parsley

2 tsp chopped fresh oregano

Makes enough for about 1 lb 2 oz/500 g meat or poultry

1 Score the meat or poultry portions deeply with a sharp knife. Put the prepared meat or poultry in a shallow nonmetallic dish or plastic food bag.

2 Put all the ingredients, except all the herbs, in a food processor or blender and process until smooth and combined. Stir in the fresh herbs.

3 Pour the marinade over the prepared meat or poultry and turn to coat.

4 Cover tightly or seal and let marinate in the refrigerator, turning occasionally, for up to 6 hours before cooking.

TASTY TIP
In Argentina and Uruguay, this marinade is used for broiled or barbecued meat, such as steak, chicken, or lamb strips, but it is also perfect for adding spice to vegetables. The flavors are a mixture of popular Spanish and Italian ingredients.

Caribbean-Style Marinade

½-inch/1-cm piece fresh ginger
root, peeled and grated

½ cup dark rum

4 tbsp freshly squeezed lime juice

4 tbsp vegetable oil

1 heaping tbsp dark brown sugar

½ tsp ground allspice

½ tsp freshly grated nutmeg

½ tsp salt

Makes enough for about
1 lb 2 oz/500 g meat, poultry,
or fish and seafood

1 Score the meat, poultry, or fish portions deeply with a sharp knife. Put the prepared meat, poultry, fish, or seafood in a shallow nonmetallic dish or plastic food bag.

2 Mix all the ingredients together in a pitcher or small bowl until thoroughly combined.

3 Pour the marinade over the prepared meat, poultry, fish, or seafood and turn to coat.

4 Cover tightly or seal and let marinate in the refrigerator, turning occasionally, for up to 2 hours before cooking.

TASTY TIP
Enjoy the exotic flavors of the Caribbean in this marinade with poultry, such as roast chicken legs, meat, pork spareribs, fish steaks, squid, and shrimp. For a sweeter marinade, use preserved ginger in syrup in place of the fresh ginger, drained and finely chopped.

Remarkable Rubs

Choose from an amazingly wide variety of spicy rub options according to your taste, from the mild Sweet Chili Rub, increasing in kick to the Jamaican Jerk Rub, to the incendiary Habanero Chile Rub. There are some well-loved standards here, such as the enticing Cajun Blackened Spice Rub and the vibrant Creole Rub, together with some intriguing combinations—unsweetened cocoa with cumin for a Mexican-style coating, or dried crushed rose petals with cinnamon for a Middle Eastern-style seasoning. In addition to other exotically fragrant recipes from Asia and North Africa, there are pungent and piquant rubs featuring fresh horseradish, citrus rind, garlic, and aromatic herbs to enliven all manner of foods, from game to seafood.

Rub the mixture into your chosen ingredients either just before cooking, if short of time, or for the length of time specified, up to 24 hours ahead, for a stronger flavor. If leaving for the maximum length of time, don't add salt until just before cooking, otherwise moisture will be drawn out of the food and the result will be dry. Use as much or as little of the rub as you wish.

BBQ Spice Rub

4 tbsp dark brown sugar

1 tbsp mustard powder

1 tbsp salt

1 tbsp pepper

2 tsp paprika

1 tsp dried thyme

1 tsp dried oregano

1 tsp cayenne pepper

1 tsp ground allspice

Makes about 9 tbsp

1 Mix all the ingredients together in a small bowl until thoroughly combined.

2 Rub the mixture thoroughly into meat, poultry, or fish just before cooking, if short of time, or up to 24 hours before cooking. If leaving for the maximum length of time, exclude the salt from the rub mixture and sprinkle over just before cooking.

3 Put in a shallow dish, cover tightly, and chill in the refrigerator until required.

TASTY TIP
This is an essential barbecue rub recipe, and is a delicious blend of spices that will add a rich, deep flavor to any meat dish, such as steaks, chops, sausages, pork chops, or spareribs. It is also particularly good when used with thick cuts of fish.

Texan-Style Rub

1 tbsp ground dried mild chiles

1 tbsp onion powder

1 tbsp mustard powder

1 tbsp ground white pepper

1 tbsp salt

Makes about 5 tbsp

1 Mix all the ingredients together in a small bowl until thoroughly combined.

2 Rub the mixture thoroughly into meat, poultry, fish, or seafood just before cooking, if short of time, or up to 24 hours before cooking. If leaving for the maximum length of time, exclude the salt from the rub mixture and sprinkle over just before cooking.

3 Put in a shallow dish, cover tightly, and chill in the refrigerator until required.

TASTY TIP
This is a tasty and mildly spicy rub that is perfectly characteristic of the flavors popular in Texas for barbecuing ribs and steaks. Remember that you can also use 2 teaspoons cayenne pepper or chili powder in place of the ground chiles.

Memphis-Style Rub

4 tbsp dark brown sugar

2 tbsp garlic powder

2 tbsp onion powder

2 tbsp celery salt

2 tbsp paprika

1 tbsp ground cumin

1 tbsp salt

2 tsp mustard powder

2 tsp dried sage

2 tsp pepper

1 tsp ground bay leaves

1 tsp cayenne pepper

Makes about 17 tbsp

1 Mix all the ingredients together in a small bowl until thoroughly combined.

2 Rub the mixture thoroughly into meat, poultry, fish, or seafood several hours, up to 24 hours, before cooking. If leaving for the maximum length of time, exclude the salt from the rub mixture and sprinkle over just before cooking.

3 Put in a shallow dish, cover tightly, and chill in the refrigerator until required.

TASTY TIP
A great combination of herbs and spices typically used in Memphis, Tennessee, where rubs are generally more popular than marinades. This is especially good with ribs, chicken, and pork. Use smoked paprika for an added flavor dimension, or use hot paprika if you want to increase the heat of the rub a degree.

Habanero Chile Rub

2 tbsp paprika

1–2 tbsp dried crushed habanero chiles or chili powder

1 tbsp garlic powder

1 tbsp onion powder

1 tbsp ground cumin

1 tbsp salt

2 tsp pepper

2 tsp light brown sugar

1 tsp cayenne pepper

1/2 tsp freshly grated nutmeg

Makes about 10 tbsp

1 Mix all the ingredients together in a small bowl until thoroughly combined.

2 Rub the mixture thoroughly into meat, poultry, fish, or seafood 1–2 hours before cooking.

3 Put in a shallow dish, cover tightly, and chill in the refrigerator until required.

TASTY TIP
This intensely hot rub will give meat, such as tasty beef and red onion kabobs, and poultry a rich, powerful, almost fruity flavor. But be warned—it is very, very hot! If you prefer, remember that you can use less chile in the recipe to create a milder rub.

Chili Espresso Rub

2 tbsp dark brown sugar

1 tbsp ground espresso coffee

1 tbsp ground coriander

2 tsp ground cumin

1 tsp ground ginger

1–2 tsp dried red chile flakes or chili powder

salt and pepper

Makes about 5 tbsp

1 Mix all the ingredients together in a small bowl until thoroughly combined.

2 Rub the mixture thoroughly into meat, poultry, fish, or seafood up to 6 hours before cooking.

3 Put in a shallow dish, cover tightly, and chill in the refrigerator until required.

TASTY TIP

The earthy, sweet hot flavors of this unusual but fabulous rub are great for meat, especially pork or beef steaks, and chicken. Use mild or hot chili according to taste. For a Mexican-style take on this rub, substitute unsweetened cocoa for the ground coffee.

Sweet Chili Rub

2 tbsp maple sugar or
light brown sugar

2 tbsp mild or medium-hot
chili powder

1 tbsp garlic powder or garlic salt

1 tbsp celery salt

1 tbsp paprika

2 tsp ground cumin

1 tsp cayenne pepper

1 tsp pepper

Makes about 8 tbsp

1 Mix all the ingredients together in a small bowl until thoroughly combined.

2 Rub the mixture thoroughly into meat, poultry, fish, or seafood several hours before cooking.

3 Put in a shallow dish, cover tightly, and chill in the refrigerator until required.

TASTY TIP
A sweet (but not too sweet) rub, it is great with meat, poultry, fish, seafood, and vegetables, such as butternut squash. Rub into corn cobs, then, when ready to cook, drizzle with a little oil or melted butter and grill over medium heat, on a barbecue or using a grill pan, for 15 minutes, or until tender.

Cajun Blackened Spice Rub

1 tbsp cracked black peppercorns

2 tsp paprika

2 tsp garlic powder or
crushed garlic

2 tsp salt

1 tsp dried thyme

1 tsp dried oregano

1 tsp mustard powder

$1/2$ tsp cayenne pepper

Makes about 4 tbsp

1 Mix all the ingredients together in a small bowl until thoroughly combined.

2 Rub the mixture thoroughly into meat, poultry, fish, or seafood just before cooking, if short of time, or for several hours before cooking.

3 Put in a shallow dish, cover tightly, and chill in the refrigerator until required.

TASTY TIP
The concept of "blackening" food was created in New Orleans. As the food cooks, the spices form a delicious caramelized crust. This recipe is excellent with meat, poultry, firm fish steaks, such as salmon or swordfish, or large shelled and deveined shrimp.

Creole Rub

2 tbsp pepper

2 tbsp celery salt

2 tbsp paprika

4 tsp garlic powder

4 tsp dried thyme

2 tsp dried oregano

2 tsp ground bay leaves

pinch of chili powder

Makes about 10 tbsp

1 Mix all the ingredients together in a small bowl until thoroughly combined.

2 Rub the mixture thoroughly into meat, poultry, fish, or seafood 1–2 hours before cooking.

3 Put in a shallow dish, cover tightly, and chill in the refrigerator until required.

TASTY TIP
This scintillating and spicy rub recipe features vibrant Creole flavors, and will really perk up your taste buds. It is particularly delicious when used with fish and seafood, so try combining it with a dish such as shrimp and monkfish cooked on skewers.

Mexican-Style Rub

4 tbsp paprika

2 tbsp ground cumin

2 tbsp light brown sugar

1 tbsp salt

4 tsp dried oregano

3 tsp unsweetened cocoa

2 tsp pepper

1–2 tsp dried red chile flakes

Makes about 13 tbsp

1 Mix all the ingredients together in a small bowl until thoroughly combined.

2 Rub the mixture thoroughly into meat, poultry, fish, or seafood 1–2 hours before cooking.

3 Put in a shallow dish, cover tightly, and chill in the refrigerator until required.

TASTY TIP
Rich, dark cocoa combines with aromatic spices to make a fantastic tasting coating for pork, beef, lamb, and poultry, such as chicken strips. Use this rub for adding flavor to strips of meat for fajitas. Brush a preheated grill pan with peanut oil and cook the meat strips over medium-high heat for 3–4 minutes on each side until cooked.

Jamaican Jerk Rub

4 tsp dark brown sugar

4 tsp chopped fresh thyme

4 tsp salt

2 tsp ground allspice

1 tsp cayenne pepper or chili powder

generous pinch of freshly grated nutmeg

pinch of ground cloves

Makes about 5 tbsp

1 Mix all the ingredients together in a small bowl until thoroughly combined.

2 Rub the mixture thoroughly into meat, poultry, fish, or seafood at least 2 hours, or up to 24 hours, before cooking. If leaving for the maximum length of time, exclude the salt from the rub mixture and sprinkle over just before cooking.

3 Put in a shallow dish, cover tightly, and chill in the refrigerator until required.

TASTY TIP
A hot, spicy rub with a definite kick from the chili powder. This is a great recipe to use with all types of meat and poultry. Try it with a whole roasted chicken. You can always reduce the amount of cayenne pepper or chili powder if you like less heat.

Dukkah Rub

1 cup hazelnuts

1/4 cup sesame seeds

1 tbsp cumin seeds

1 tbsp coriander seeds

3–4 black peppercorns

1 tsp salt

Makes about 5 tbsp

1 Put the hazelnuts in a heavy-bottomed skillet and cook over medium-high heat, shaking the skillet frequently, for 3–4 minutes until toasted and golden. Tip out of the skillet and let cool.

2 Add all the seeds and peppercorns to the skillet and toast in the same way. Tip out of the skillet and let cool.

3 Put the toasted hazelnuts, seeds, and peppercorns with the salt in a food processor or electric grinder and process or grind briefly until crushed to a coarse powder. Don't process or grind for too long, otherwise the spices will become oily.

4 Rub the mixture thoroughly into meat, poultry, fish, or seafood at least 1 hour before cooking.

5 Put in a shallow dish, cover tightly, and chill in the refrigerator until required.

TASTY TIP
This crumbly blend of spices and hazelnuts (or sometimes ground dried chickpeas) originated in Egypt. Use with meat, poultry, and fish. It is especially tasty with lamb and chicken. Toast other types of nuts, such as blanched almonds, raw cashews, or skinned pistachios, in place of the hazelnuts.

North African-Style Rub

1 tbsp cloves

1 tbsp black peppercorns

1 tbsp ground coriander

2 tsp ground cinnamon

1 tsp freshly grated nutmeg

1/2 tsp cayenne pepper

Makes about 4 tbsp

1 Put the cloves and peppercorns in a food processor or electric grinder and process or grind briefly until crushed to a coarse powder. Don't process or grind for too long, otherwise the spices will become oily. Stir in the remaining ingredients.

2 Rub the mixture thoroughly into meat, poultry, fish, or seafood at least 4 hours before cooking.

3 Put in a shallow dish, cover tightly, and chill in the refrigerator until required.

TASTY TIP
An aromatic, exotic-tasting rub that is used in North Africa to flavor vegetables and lamb. Use the rub to pep up strips of vegetables before drizzling with oil and roasting in a preheated oven at 400°F/200°C, turning occasionally, for 25 minutes, or until tender and browned.

Asian Spice Rub

4 tbsp sesame seeds, toasted

1/2-inch/1-cm piece fresh
ginger root, peeled and grated

1 tbsp ground turmeric

2 tsp jaggery or light brown sugar

1 tsp salt

1 tsp ground coriander

1/2 tsp ground cardamom seeds

1/2 tsp ground cumin

1/2 tsp ground cinnamon

1/2 tsp pepper

Makes about 7 tbsp

1 Mix all the ingredients together in a small bowl until thoroughly combined.

2 Rub the mixture thoroughly into meat, poultry, fish, or seafood at least 4 hours before cooking.

3 Put in a shallow dish, cover tightly, and chill in the refrigerator until required.

TASTY TIP
A lively, aromatic mixture of popular Asian spices. Use for all types of meat, poultry (especially duck), and firm cuts of fish, such as tuna and swordfish steaks. Jaggery, also called palm sugar, is a dark unrefined sugar with a fragrant flavor and can be found in specialist and Asian food stores.

Szechuan Peppercorn Rub

2 tbsp Szechuan peppercorns

2 tbsp coriander seeds

1 tsp allspice berries

1 tsp salt

Makes about 5 tbsp

1 Put the Szechuan peppercorns and coriander seeds in a heavy-bottomed skillet and cook over medium-high heat, shaking the skillet frequently, for 2 minutes, or until their fragrance is released. Tip out of the skillet and let cool, discarding any Szechuan peppercorns that have blackened.

2 Put the toasted Szechuan peppercorns and coriander seeds with the allspice berries and salt in a food processor or electric grinder and process or grind briefly until crushed to a coarse powder. Don't process or grind for too long, otherwise the spices will become oily.

3 Rub the mixture thoroughly into meat, poultry, fish, or seafood at least 2 hours before cooking.

4 Put in a shallow dish, cover tightly, and chill in the refrigerator until required.

TASTY TIP
Szechuan peppercorns have a pronounced spicy, woody aroma and are excellent with meat and poultry, especially duck. Szechuan peppercorns are not related to black and white peppercorns but are in fact small red berries that are dried. Toasting the berries releases their aromatic oils.

Star Anise and Cinnamon Rub

2 tbsp whole star anise

1 tbsp black peppercorns

2 tbsp light brown sugar

2 tsp salt

1 heaping tsp ground cinnamon

Makes about 6 tbsp

1 Put the star anise and peppercorns in an electric grinder and grind briefly until crushed to a coarse powder. Don't process or grind for too long, otherwise the spices will become oily. Stir in the remaining ingredients.

2 Rub the mixture thoroughly into meat, poultry, fish, or seafood a few hours before cooking.

3 Put in a shallow dish, cover tightly, and chill in the refrigerator until required.

TASTY TIP
The rich flavor of star anise is combined here with the sweet fragrance of cinnamon and the heat of black pepper. It is a good rub for meat, such as pork. The ground anise and peppercorns are teamed with other ground spices, usually cloves, cassia bark, fennel seed, and Szechuan peppercorns, to form Chinese five-spice powder.

Rose and Spice Rub

2 tbsp dried crushed rose petals

2 tbsp ground cinnamon

1 tbsp ground cardamom seeds

1 tbsp ground turmeric

1 tsp ground cloves

1 tsp freshly grated nutmeg

1 tsp pepper

Makes about 7 tbsp

1 Mix all the ingredients together in a small bowl until thoroughly combined.

2 Rub the mixture thoroughly into meat, poultry, fish, or seafood at least 2 hours before cooking.

3 Put in a shallow dish, cover tightly, and chill in the refrigerator until required.

TASTY TIP
Sweetly scented rose petals add an extra dimension to the flavor of this fragrant rub, which is particularly good with chicken, duck, and lamb. Look for dried rose petals in specialist food stores or purchase from Middle Eastern food suppliers.

Ras el Hanout

2 tsp ground cumin

2 tsp ground ginger

2 tsp ground turmeric

2 tsp ground cinnamon

2 tsp ground cardamom seeds

2 tsp ground coriander seeds

2 tsp ground ginger

2 tsp ground allspice

2 tsp saffron threads

1 tsp freshly grated nutmeg

1 tsp salt

1 tsp pepper

1/2 tsp ground cloves

Makes about 7 tbsp

1 Mix all the ingredients together in a small bowl until thoroughly combined.

2 Rub the mixture thoroughly into meat, poultry, fish, or seafood just before cooking.

3 Put in a shallow dish, cover tightly, and chill in the refrigerator until required.

TASTY TIP
The name of this fragrant blend of Moroccan spices literally means "top of the shop"—the best spices in the store. Use for meat and poultry, especially lamb, chicken, and duck, as well as fish, seafood, and vegetables, such as onion and sweet potato wedges or zucchini.

Garlic and Horseradish Rub

2 garlic cloves, finely chopped

2 tbsp olive oil

2 tbsp freshly grated horseradish root

1 tbsp Dijon mustard

1 tbsp dark brown sugar

$^1/_2$ tsp pepper

$^1/_2$ tsp salt

Makes about 8 tbsp

1 Mix all the ingredients together in a small bowl until thoroughly combined.

2 Rub the mixture thoroughly into meat, poultry, fish, or seafood 1–2 hours before cooking.

3 Put in a shallow nonmetallic dish, cover tightly, and chill until required. The rub can be made ahead, stored in an airtight container, and refrigerated for up to 3 days.

TASTY TIP
A hot, pungent rub that will add heat to meat, and is best cooked with roast beef, game, and poultry. The sugar in the recipe softens the tang of the horseradish. If you prefer a hotter rub, you can always substitute some English mustard instead of the Dijon.

Greek-Style Rub

finely grated rind of 1 lemon

2 tbsp dried oregano

1 tbsp dried thyme

1 tbsp dried rosemary

1 tsp garlic powder

¹/₂ tsp pepper

¹/₂ tsp salt

Makes about 6 tbsp

1 Mix all the ingredients together in a small bowl until thoroughly combined.

2 Rub the mixture thoroughly into meat, poultry, fish, or seafood 3–4 hours before cooking.

3 Put in a shallow nonmetallic dish, cover tightly, and refrigerate until required.

TASTY TIP

This highly aromatic herb rub is fabulous with lamb, but also goes well with other meats, poultry, firm white fish steaks, and vegetables. Try with eggplants. Rub into the cut sides of thickly sliced eggplant. Brush a preheated grill pan with oil and cook over medium-high heat, turning once, for 10 minutes until browned.

Mediterranean Herb Rub

finely grated rind of 1 orange

finely grated rind of 1 lemon

3 garlic cloves, crushed

4 tbsp chopped fresh rosemary

2 tbsp chopped fresh sage

1 tbsp chopped fresh thyme

1 tbsp salt

2 tsp pepper

Makes about 10 tbsp

1 Mix all the ingredients together in a small bowl until thoroughly combined.

2 Rub the mixture thoroughly into meat, poultry, fish, or seafood, at least 2 hours, up to 24 hours, before cooking. If leaving for the maximum length of time, exclude the salt from the rub mixture and sprinkle over just before cooking.

3 Put in a shallow nonmetallic dish, cover tightly, and refrigerate until required.

TASTY TIP
The fresh, bold flavors of the aromatic herbs and citrus rind in this recipe make this a perfect rub for use with all types of meat, poultry, fish, and seafood, such as whole seabass, squid, and scallops. It is also a delicious way to add interest to your vegetables.

Index